The Power In A Vision Driven Family

The Journey To A Generational Vision

Phillip S. Porter, M.B.A.
Janice Williams-Porter, M.S., Ed.S.
Vanessa N. Patterson, B.A.
Vonzella Love Watson, M.S., L.M.F.T.

GENERATIONS UNITED, LLC
Publishers

Title ID: 5835047
ISBN-13: 978-1533552983
ISBN-10: 1533552983

Generations United, LLC
Email: visiondrivenfamily@gmail.com
Facebook: www.facebook.com/Visiondrivenfamily
Website: www.gunitedone.wix.com/phillipjaniceporter

Dedication

This book is dedicated to the powerful visionaries who inspired this book Rev. Dr. James Porter, Deaconess Barbara Jean Lambert Porter and our ancestors who went before us.

In Loving Memory of

Rev. Edward L. Love

Barbara Jean Lambert Porter

Rev. Dr. James Porter, Sr.

Marilynn Antoinette Williams Wells

Elvalene Magee Williams

Willie Lethell Williams, Sr.

Acknowledgements

A heart-felt thanks to Mable Hewitt, Dr. Hilliard L. Lackey and Lillian Troupe Lackey, Min. Marian E. Love, Rev. Fred D. Moore, Dr. Ellington W. Porter, Sr., James Porter, III, Phillip O. Porter, and Ron Porter and for wisdom, leadership, knowledge, love and spirit filled passion to share the importance of having an inspirational family vision. Thank you for being examples of Godly representatives that we respect, admire and emulate. We greatly appreciate your continued support and for writing an excellent foreword for this book.

Special thanks to our friends and colleagues for your professional editing skills and hard-work. We could not have published this book without your assistance. We appreciate the commitment of our editors Carlene Williams, Director of Communications, Generations United, LLC and Yvette Turner, Educator in Minneapolis, Minnesota.

Phillip & Janice Porter

We would like to thank our family business Generations United, LLC for praying, supporting, marketing, promoting and publishing this book. A special thank you to Generations United board members Servia Fortenberry, Mable Hewitt, Ron Porter, Marilynn Wells, Phillip Wells, and Brenda Williams.

Vanessa Norwood Patterson

Thanks to my Co-Authors Phillip and Janice Porter for being resilient and obedient to your calling in this season. I am grateful to my uncles Herman Norwood, Leroy Norwood, Richard Norwood, Henry Norwood, T.J. Norwood and Samuel Norwood for carrying out the vision of my Grandfather, Henry Norwood.

Thanks most of all to Dr. James and Mother Barbara Porter for your teachings on vision, unity and family.

Vonzella Love Watson

I'd like to offer special thanks to co-authors Philip and Janice Porter and to Vanessa Patterson for continuing to press for the mark and being so resilient and steadfast. I would also like to thank my parents Betty Jean Love and Reverend Edward Love for raising nine children and teach them the ways of the Lord. I also want to thank Reverend James Porter and Mother Barbara Porter because this could not have happened without their vision. Certainly I thank Generations United.

Foreword

HERE IS A BOOK THAT GIVES PRACTICAL, REALISTIC AND BASIC STEPS TO SOLVE THE AGE OLD PROBLEM MANY FAMILIES HAVE ON HOW TO LIFT THEMSELVES OUT OF GENERATIONAL POVERTY.

It requires forward thinking, by not concentrating on your present circumstances such as lack of finances, education, race, gender, in other words, **excuses** for not putting into action the steps set forth in this book. (*For God hath not given us the spirit of fear; but of power, and of love, and of a sound mind 2 Timothy 1:7*)

Keep in mind this is their family story and how God revealed Himself to them simply because they **asked**, had enough **faith** and **trust** to take the necessary walk with God through this process. (*God never asks us to do something that he will not carry us through step by step.*) Each step written in this book is inspired by this family's obedience to Him who is The Great "I AM".

As I read this book it reminded me of the many favored people in the Bible who stepped out on faith, knocked down whatever giants crossed their path, (*like not having participation from every family member*) but kept their eye on the goal and did receive the prize. This book helps us to remember that great things can happen today.

Thank goodness God knows the authors' hearts and minds. He knew they would unselfishly share their knowledge of God's laws of abundance with this now confident, well-written book. Take it to heart. Use it as a study guide. This family knows He is not a God of 'lack'. (Eph. 3:20), (John 10:10)

If I seem passionate about this book it is because I know

the history of this family and I can see the generational progress and growth they have made and will continue to make in the future because they have set forth a worthy **vision** and a clear cut, solid **plan** to live in abundance according to His Riches in Heaven.(Phil. 4:19)

Min. Marian E. Love (Facebook)
Marian Love (Google)
BA Liberal Arts
BA El. Education (K-8)
Love Productions Dedicated to Arts and Education

∞∞∞∞

Being a child growing up and witnessing the early stages of the vision of Rev. Dr. James and Barbara Porter, Sr. come to life was a journey in itself. It's a powerful thing to be able to use the power of God, education, determination and focus to achieve the vision Grandpa and Grandma had those many years ago. I didn't truly understand what the whole fuss was about until uncle Phil first revealed the family vision which included Generations United and ask me to design the first logo. Then it all came rushing to me at the same time! Generations Uniting! The concept was so clear. A family that prays together not only stays together but also creates prosperity together. #JTTO

James Porter, III
GEN 3

∞∞∞∞

Wow! Phillip, Janice, Vonzella and Vanessa, great work. This is a must read account. Very much a reminder of our "core vision" and a "blue print" for success. This book is full of helpful tools for planning, building, mending, healing, moving and strengthening the family. Straight ahead and deliberately. Just a great reminder of the power of prayer. Reading this account reminds me of the many business meetings, prayer times, task assignments, and brainstorming sessions. Thanks so very much for pointing the way, "both our families" are worth it.

May this book encourage "many" families to grow exponentially in strength, love, caring and sharing. The vision is so clear. Truly there is more than one way to share the deep love of Christ with friends and family.

Micah 6:8 in the Message (MSG) bible says it this way: But he's already made it plain how to live, what to do, what God is looking for in men and women. It's quite simple: Do what is fair and just to your neighbor, be compassionate and loyal in your love, And don't take yourself too seriously— take God seriously.

Ron Porter, M.B.A.
Generations United, LLC
Executive Vice President
Board Member
GEN 2

Initially, when I heard the suggestion that our family the Williams/Magee might merge with the Porter/Lambert family, I thought that was a great idea. Although, I didn't fully grasp the depths of what this could mean at that time, I was excited about the proposal.

As the oldest child of Willie Lethell and Elvalene Magee-Williams, I remember a long time ago my sister Janice telling me about how Phillip and his family saved money and how they helped each other. In our family, we were taught to save 10% of our money. However, we were never taught how to save money collectively as a family for future generations. The impact of this merger has enriched the lives of our entire family. If we learned this powerful concept, so can you. Reading this book helped me to realize the significance of coming together on one accord and working towards a common vision that benefits future generations.

Finally, hearing about the land investment was an even greater idea. Phillip and I talked about how to merge the family and how to become a board member of Generations United. The merger of our two families has been beneficial and will continue to enhance the lives of future generations.

Mable Hewitt, Williams/Magee Family Matriarch
Generations United, LLC
President Family Legacy Division
Board Member
GEN 2

When we think of the essence and strength of family in the 21st century context, it can have a meaning that is as complex as the landscape of this culture in which we live. I believe that this book serves as a manual that brings clarity to what the definition of family is all about. Though all of the writers are not necessarily related by DNA, they have a common core belief system that brings them into a place that empowers, strengthens, and emboldens them to continue their legacy forward on to future generations. This is what family is all about.

It is my personal belief that if you do not know your history, your future will be a mystery. Phillip, Janice, Vanessa, and Vonzella through this book, give us significant family history by sharing stories of historical dreams that impacted their lives through their parents', even before they were a mere figment of their parents' imagination. The writers also show the readers various strategies that have taken these dreams to a living reality that have produced both prosperity and posterity.

I can personally testify that my Uncle James and Aunt Barbara Porter were leaders of legacy. They always encouraged me to go after my dreams of being the best musician, preacher, and pastor. Not only did they encourage me, but also they sowed seed into my life. I remember as a youth I would travel every summer with my father, Dr. Robert Porter, to Greater Friendship in Minneapolis, Minnesota for the summer revival he would preach. After the week would end, my Uncle would hand me a basket, and have me stand down in the front of the church, and he would speak words of encouragement and life over me, and then he would encourage the congregation to bring a love offering and sow it into my future. As a teenager I was super "juiced" (excited) to get some money. But, as I grew older I realized that what my Uncle and Auntie did was an investment in my future.

When my father passed away in 1999, my brother, Dr. Tecoy Porter, Sr., and I took the helm of pastorship of the Genesis Missionary Baptist Church. The Sunday after the funeral, Pastor James Porter, stood as Uncle, Pastor, and Leader of Porter Legacy and told the church these are your pastors, and encouraged them to follow our leadership as God leads us. Dr. J. Porter took us and poured knowledge into us, reminding us that though we hadn't been to school for Theology, or ministerial training yet, God was with us to win. He reminded us that we were from a legacy of pastors, stretching now three generations. Lastly, he sowed into us by investing finances into our Pastoral robes, and books for training.

I am grateful that this book, which is more like a manual, has been birthed and is being released to the nations. I implore and encourage you to read it, digest it, and implement it. Become a leader of legacy as you read and learn about "***The Power In A Vision Driven Family.***"

Dr. Ellington W. Porter, Sr.
Sr. Pastor Genesis Church
Sacramento, CA

Phillip S. Porter, Janice M. Williams-Porter, Vanessa N. Patterson, Vonzella Love Watson have put together a masterpiece entitled **The Power In A Vision Driven Family:** *The Journey To A Generational Vision!* As we the undersign approach our Golden Anniversary of marriage (1966-2016), we salute the authors and add one or two bits of wisdom supportive of this wonderful book.

First and foremost, we consider marriage as a fortress for well-being. Marriage should be the uniting of families not a source of dissension or contention. Eloping or marrying against or without the consent of four biological living parents is essentially a no-no. The love the couple have for themselves ought to expand to the love of both sets of parents and to the extent feasible, to the accompanying relatives. The Biblical story of Ruth is a shining example of God's blessings upon the coming together of in-laws.

We also believe in holy matrimony. Marriage under this rubric begins in prayer and may continue under the guise of "The family that prays together stays together."

Not only that, who among us does not say grace at each and every meal? If we invoke blessings upon the food we are about to receive, then surely we should solicit blessings upon the child we are about to conceive. At the risk of divulging too much personal information, we prayerfully planned the conception of our children down to the minutest detail.

We learned that from 1 Samuel 1:27-28 which reads:

> She said, "Oh, my lord! As your soul lives, my lord, I am the woman who stood here beside you, praying to the LORD. 27"For this boy I prayed, and the LORD has given me my petition which I asked of Him. 28"So I have also dedicated him to the LORD; as long as he

lives he is dedicated to the LORD." And he worshiped the LORD there.

Thus, we endorse and highly recommend **The Power In A Vision Driven Family:** *The Journey To A Generational Vision!* The Baha'i Faith says marriage has the singular potential to strengthen the social fabric of society, to knit closer the ties of the home, to place a certain gratitude and respect in the hearts of the children for those who have given them life and sent their souls out on the eternal journey towards their Creator. Finally, the Unification Church of South Korea contends that marriages can unite the world. Then, surely the union of these two unlikely families in this wonderful book is a step in that direction.

Dr. Hilliard L. Lackey and Lillian Troupe Lackey

In order to make a forest, you must first plant trees...This was a saying I always lived by, so once my uncle handed me this manuscript, I was enthralled by the content. I am honored to get this first class ticket into the mind of a visionary, a step by step guide... you could say, to assist in molding generations.

In order to build a great foundation, you must have the best concrete to base your structure. This book gives you the tools to build a dynasty, to form a network with your family, and to reach any level desired. If this is your ambition, then I implore you to pick up **The Power In A Vision Driven Family**...it's an inspiration to read! I loved it!!

Phillip O. Porter
GEN 3

ชช ชช ชช ชช

Rev. Dr. James and Mrs. Barbara Porter have captured the minds and hearts of many by guiding them to an enlightenment of the need to commit early to sacrificial type endeavors. Their way of life exemplifies an unwavering obligation to God. The Bible says the steps of a good man are ordered by God, indicating that his work will be favored by the one who led him to it. The Porters' vision is not hampered by things that commonly hinder many, such as procrastination, lack of fortitude, and no sense of holding on. As a result, their success is claimed in these pages by their faith, their discipline, their dignity, and their upward mobility of determination.

The Porters leave for many, a legacy; not just an inheritance, but a name changing, life changing, and mind changing experience for those who will read and connect themselves to this awesome labor. Richer are we for the experience we will gain from this read. I suggest to our readers that we are stronger when we bind our tides. I, too, can identify with mountain climbing journeys and treacherous turns. The benefits of holding on outweigh the inflexibility of the climb.

May God shine on all those who shared in this work, may he keep you in perfect peace until your next journey.

Rev. Fred D. Moore
Pastor and Author
Christian Chapel Baptist
Demopolis, Alabama
Author
The Pregnant Pulpit

TABLE OF CONTENTS

Preface

Where there is no vision, the people perish: but he that keepeth the law, happy is he.

Proverbs 29:18 KJV

We believe as you read this book, you will be driven to implement your own vision for your family. We believe an energizing vision will give your family a purpose, increase trust, improve communication that will lead to increased spiritual, physical and financial wealth of your family, community and the world.

When people hear about the accomplishments of our family and that our family achievements are a direct result of our family vision, generally we get the following questions:

1. How did you create your family vision?

2. How did you get your family to listen and support your family vision?

3. Was it hard to implement your family vision for so many years?

These questions are part of the primary reason we wrote this book. Our desire was to provide an easy guide or road map for families by sharing authentic examples from our family. This "how- to" guide will help thousands of families create, implement and maintain their own transformative family vision; which will positively impact the family, and their community for generations.

This book is a detailed account of the family vision of Rev. Dr. James and Barbara Jean Lambert-Porter, Sr. from the moment their dream was conceived to when their family vision was successfully transferred to the next generation. It spans over 40 years of their life from 1972 through 2013 when they went home to be with the Lord.

This book was written from the personal experiences and view point of Phillip S. Porter and Janice M. Williams-Porter. Phillip is the third and youngest son of James and Barbara Jean Lambert Porter. Janice M. Williams-Porter is the wife of Phillip. After many years of "kitchen table" conversations with our parents, we decided to write this book to inform and educate individuals and families of our global communities:

- To provide a proven road map to use as a guide to create, implement, maintain and transfer their family's vision successfully to the next generation.

- To encourage and motivate families to take action because it doesn't matter whether your family is poor, average and ordinary or wealthy; your family will receive life changing benefits from a family vision.

- To share the journey of our family experiences in order to establish our family vision in hopes that it will inspire you to take action today to create and implement a vision for your family.

- To share the powerful impact that our family vision has had on our family today.

- To inform family leaders and help them understand that implementing a family vision may be difficult but the family generational benefits are worth the sacrifices. The benefits will go beyond your wildest imagination.

We believe this book is unique because rarely will you find an example of an African American family who has a written family vision and mission statement which can be clearly articulated by several generations. We are blessed to be the son and daughter of visionary parents in Rev. Dr. James & Barbara Jean Lambert Porter. As visionary parents, they:

- **Asked** God for an inspirational family vision that will impact future generations.
- **Received** God's vision for their family and immediately took action.
- **Established** a formal process for implementing their family vision.
- **Created** a clear inspirational vision and mission statement for their family.
- **Successfully communicated** and **transferred** their family vision into the hearts and minds of the next two generations before they went home to be with the Lord in 2013.
- **Understood** and **accepted** their role in the family vision. Like Moses, God allowed them to see their promise land in Colorado while knowing and accepting the fact that they would never live on the land.

In this book, we shared how the purchase of a few acres of vacant land in Colorado by our parents was transformed over a 40 year period into an awesome "Big Audacious Family Vision" to create a family "home place" and resort in Colorado, Texas and Sierra Leone, West Africa. God expanded their family vision to include the merger of two unlikely African American families from different regions of the United States.

We have included as the final chapter of this book a section where you can write your own family vision and mission statement and begin sharing it with your family. The journey to establish or expand your family dream, vision and mission begins today.

To best understand this book we have provided a profile of our parents, the visionaries.

Rev. Dr. James Porter, Sr. was born to Nettie (White) and Vivian Ellington Porter on January 5, 1930 in Kansas City, Kansas. James Porter was the seventh of thirteen children. He attended Sumner High School an African American school in Kansas City, Kansas. He met and fell in love with

Barbara Jean Lambert while attending Sumner High School. He later married Barbara on May 1, 1949.

Rev. Dr. James Porter was ordained in 1957 under the leadership of his father, Rev. Vivian Ellington Porter. He received a 2 year certificate in Theology at Calvary Bible College and National College in Kansas City, MO. He received a Bachelor of Arts degree in Sociology and worked toward his

Masters in Sociology at the University of Missouri at Kansas City. He received his Masters of Arts degree in Teaching at Converse College in Spartanburg, South Carolina. He received his Bachelor of Theology and Bachelor of Divinity degrees from Teamer Religious and Educational Enterprises, Inc. of Charlotte, North Carolina. He received his Honorary Doctorate of Law Degree from Cuyahoga College in Cleveland, Ohio. He earned his Doctorate of Ministry Degree from the United Theological Seminary, New Brighton, MN.

He pastored the following churches:

- New Hope Missionary Baptist Church, Kansas City, Missouri
- New Hope Missionary Baptist Church, St. Joseph, Missouri
- Bethlehem Missionary Baptist Church, Simpsonville, South Carolina
- Bruton Temple Missionary Baptist Church, Greenville,

South Carolina
- Shiloh Baptist Church, Anderson, South Carolina
- Greater Friendship Missionary Baptist Church, Minneapolis, Minnesota
- St. John's Missionary Baptist Church, Longview, Texas.

In addition to being a visionary, he was a pastor, author, writer, teacher, counselor, mentor, community spokesman, and recognized leader throughout the United States. He went home to be with our Heavenly Father on October 19, 2013.

 **Barbara Jean Lambert Porter** was born to Anna Belle and Richard Lambert, Sr. on June 25, 1930 in Kansas City, Kansas. Barbara was the eldest of two children. Barbara Jean began her walk with God at the age of 13 by confessing Jesus Christ as her Lord and

Savior. She attended Sumner High School in Kansas City, Kansas. She met and fell in love with James Porter whom she later married on May 1, 1949. In their 64 years of marriage, they were blessed with 3 children, 14 grandchildren and 23 great-grandchildren.

Barbara was a deaconess, mother, prayer warrior, registered nurse, teacher, mentor and a trusted leader in her community and throughout the United States. She went home to be with our Heavenly Father on May 1, 2013.

Introduction

Does your family have a clear inspiring vision or purpose? Have you formally shared your dream in writing with your family? Do you or the leaders in your family know how to establish a motivating vision for your family? When you attend your family reunions or family holiday gatherings, does your family joyfully recite the family vision and mission statements? Are your personal and career goals intertwined with your family's vision? Did you further your education after high school in a field that would benefit your family? Are you working in a job where your training, skills and experiences will noticeably enhance your family's knowledge and economic status? Are you willing to make personal sacrifices for the greater good of future generations?

If you answered no to any of these questions, this book is for you and your family.

When we started writing this book, we administered an informal survey. The survey was only one question with a response of yes or no. The survey was administered to our social network on Facebook, LinkedIn and email database. We asked the following question: "Does your family have a formal written vision and mission statement?" We had 93 people to respond to our survey and from those 93 people, 91.2% answered **no** and 8.8% answered **yes**. This is an alarming statistic. We are on a journey to increase the number of families throughout the world who have an inspirational written family vision and mission.

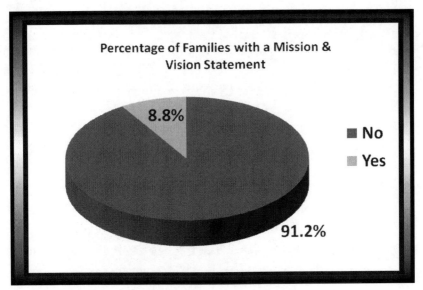

Figure 1.0 Families with Vision & Mission Statement

Reading this book is your first step to moving out of the 91% into the upper 9% joining the families with a vision and mission statement. We have revealed the secrets to creating your family vision and the journey required to make your vision come true for your family. We recommend that you read this book with your family because together you will learn:

- How to create, implement and maintain an inspiring vision and mission statement for your family.

- The benefits of establishing a motivating family vision.

- Fifteen great tips on how to implement a motivating family vision.

- Why having 100% immediate buy-in of your family member is not a requirement to implement your stimulating family vision.

- The length of time it takes to establish your family vision will be different because each family is different.

Our hope is that you and your family will stop procrastinating and implement your family vision today. We sincerely believe the more families that have a family vision, the stronger the family and a better quality of life for all. A successful family vision will satisfy the inner and economic needs of both the individual and family.

Now turn to chapter one "Dream Seeds Planted in Colorado" and begin your visionary journey.

Chapter 1

Dream Seed Planted In Colorado

Date	Family Milestones
2/15/1972	James & Barbara Jean "Lambert" Porter planted their dream seed with the purchase of vacant land in Colorado
6/21/1972	James & Barbara Jean "Lambert" Porter planted more dream seeds with the purchase of additional vacant land in Colorado
3/21/1987	James & Barbara Jean "Lambert" Porter planted even more dreams seeds with the purchase of additional vacant land in Colorado

James Porter and Barbara Jean Lambert were married at the age of 19 and 18 respectively, on May 1, 1949 in Kansas City. From this day forward, they were excited about their future and were looking forward to starting a family. In Barbara Jean Lambert Porter's own words, "as a Christian Negro Couple who grew up and experienced racism, we believed that racism was no match for the great things God had in store for us". They believed with God all things were possible and that together they would achieve wonderful things for their family. Since the day they were married, it was their dream that their children, grandchildren and future generations would have a better quality of life. This quality of life would be based on their moral character, education, knowledge, and strong work ethics and not solely based on the color of their skin and strength of their "back". These characteristics were the core value established for our family. These solid core values would be the foundation on which their family vision were later built. James and Barbara Porter knew that if their family was to achieve their God given destiny, they must establish a clear family vision based on their strongly held core values. However, they knew that establishing a clear family generational vision was not enough unless their vision was faithfully received by at least their children and grandchildren. The challenge before them was to conceive and make visible an inspiring multi-generational family vision.

During the next twenty years, James and Barbara while going about their daily lives of working full-time, rearing three sons, attending college, pastoring churches, and more, they continued to ask God to give them a vision for their family that would expand generations. After many years, in 1972 God planted a dream seed in their hearts.

On February 15, 1972, while vacationing in Colorado at the age of 42 years young, God placed His vision in their spirit. This vision lives on now in their offspring. The action they took on that day would later be the single most important decision of their life. It was transformative! It changed the direction of their family for generations. This was the day James and Barbara Jean Lambert Porter purchased their first 5 acres of vacant land in Colorado. When they saw this land, God immediately placed in their hearts the desire to purchase this land. This strong desire was immediately followed by weighing the pros and cons of purchasing this land.

There were two practical reasons for purchasing this vacant property, shelter and food. Dad always said that "shelter was

2

important because when hard times come and they will come with land you will always have a place to park your car, pitch your tent and sleep at night." Then for food, "you will always have a place to plant some vegetables and put food in your belly".

On the other hand, there were many obvious disadvantages to buying this land. First, common sense was telling them, "we can't afford to buy this land because you are barely making it now". Second, this land as good as it is, was located 675 miles from your home in Kansas City. Who in their right mind is going to buy land 675 miles from home? Third, most of their friends and family will think they are crazy to buy this land so far from Kansas City. If they want vacant land, it would make more sense to buy it closer to home. Fourth, they don't have any money saved to build a house on the land.

In spite of all the disadvantages there was one overwhelming factor, their strong belief that God was telling them to buy this land. So with that, they stepped out on faith at the age of 42 and purchased the land. Buying this land was a major life decision for a married couple, born and raised during the depression and segregation. In their own might and limited resources they could not afford it but they knew with Christ all things are possible. They believed that since God gave them the desire to buy the land, God also had a reason. Now it was their job to have faith and buy the land.

Rev. James & Barbara Porter purchased the land. It was their dream to establish a safe haven for hard times ahead for themselves, their children, grandchildren and great-grandchildren. This would also be the place for family reunions, holiday gatherings and more. Since their family is filled with ministers, musicians, singers, etc. it would have a recording studio. This would be a place where we could design a Christian school for the community. So over the next few years, they planted their dream seeds with the purchase of 28 acres of beautiful scenic land in Colorado.

The purchase of this land in Colorado was a tremendous personal sacrifice. They spent the next 10 plus years paying on the land. They did not miss a payment because they believed their family's future depended on it. Each year, they paid the property taxes on time as well. Every few years for over 40 years, they would make time to travel to Colorado to check on the property to make sure there were no squatters or cows grazing on the land. One year they found animals grazing on the land and as a result they put up a fence to secure the property. Visiting their land was not always easy and convenient. When they moved to South Carolina their land was 1,578 miles away yet they visited their dream land. Their move to Minneapolis, Minnesota put them 1,138 miles from their property in Colorado and yet they found a way to visit their dream land. Their move to Texas put them 817 miles away from Colorado and they continued to find a way to visit their dream land. Each time they visited their land, God renewed their dream and expanded their vision for their family. With each visit came a refreshed anointing of God's vision in their life.

The first step of James and Barbara's dream was in place with the purchase of the land in Colorado. Now it was time to move into phase two by starting a family investment club. In 1987, they launched the family savings and investment club.

Have you asked God for a life changing family vision?

Secret Steps To Creating Our iFamily Vision
1st: Asked God for an "iFamily Vision" that will expand generations.
2nd: Established family's key core beliefs and values.
3rd: Purchased vacant land in Colorado.

Vision Tips
Tip 1: Establish a grand family vision that is big enough for each individual member and the entire family.
Tip 2: Have enough faith in God & your dream to take action today even if you have to do it by yourself.
Tip 3: Do not procrastinate take action towards your dream today and set an example for your family.
Tip 4: A grand family vision is not achieved without great personal sacrifice.

Our Thoughts, Desire, Vision and Prayer

And the Lord answered me and said, write the vision, and make it plain upon tables, that he may run that readeth it. For the vision is yet for an appointed time, but at the end it shall speak and not lie: though it tarry wait for it; because it will surely come, it will not tarry.
Habakkuk 2:2-3 KJV

We desired better for our family

Commit your work to the Lord and your plans will be established.
Proverbs 16:3

We petitioned the Lord for clarity and understanding of the desire and vision.

For I know the plans I have for you that you may prosper and not for evil to give you a future and a hope.
Jeremiah 29:11

Our thought turned into desire,
Our desire became a God given vision,
Our vision required action and sacrifice,
Prayer, faith and belief were the prerequisite for our legacy to be birthed.

By
Vanessa Patterson

Family Member Testimonial

Our family vision focuses the entire family on a common goal and teaches the younger generation the value of the legacy being built for them.

Our family vision energizes the younger generations and gives them hope and believes that through our family we achieve greatness. I believe our system is better than "The Man's" system. We have experienced increased communication between the family members. Family members are now working together and helping each other.

To me Generations United long-term mission is to provide family leaders with proven resources and tools that will bring their family closer together. Then assist family leaders in taking the next generation to a higher level.

Phillip Wells, Retired Marine
Chief Operating Officer
Vice President Military Division
Generations United Board Member
GEN 2

Chapter 2

Investment Club Accumulating Cash

Date	Family Milestones
3/1/1987	Founded Family Savings & Investment Club as a Partnership in Minneapolis, Minnesota
5/1/1987	Family members began investing a minimum of $25.00/month

In 1987 Rev. James and Barbara Porter were now 57 years young and they determined it was time to move the family into phase II of their family legacy vision. As the proud owners of 28 acres of vacant land in Colorado, they now needed a plan that would generate enough cash to build and maintain a home on their property. After much discussion and research, they decided to start a family investment club. Starting an investment club was challenging because they did not have any investment experience. Additionally, they did not have any discretionary income to lose in the stock market. However, they knew they could overcome these obstacles by learning the strategies for investing in mutual funds and stocks. They chose to make some personal sacrifices, like work extra overtime and eat more beans, rice and cornbread in order to have a little money to invest each month. This was the beginning of their family's first investment club.

Under Barbara's leadership, the family entered phase two of their dream launching their first family investment club on March 1, 1987. The investment club was a partnership comprised of the nuclear family members who had a desire to participate. The key was the **desire** to participate. She knew that when it came to money, all investments must be voluntary. Her wisdom and mindset was astounding: She knew it wasn't crucial that every family member participate because achieving their dream wasn't dependent on any one person. Each nuclear family member was asked to invest $25.00 per month. Before Rev. James and Barbara Porter started the investment club, they were 100% committed to investing their money even if no other family member invested. Around the time of their anniversary May 1, 1987, several family members who had the desire to invest began investing in the family savings and investment club. Their family investment club was founded on the premise that each family member invested their money with no intention of withdrawing it for at least 10 years. This money was to be used to fulfill the needs of the family not an individual family member. The expectation and understanding agreed upon was that each family member invested their money for at least 10 years knowing that investing in stocks were risky business.

To start a family investment club, the family did the following:

Step 1 Cash Accumulation: The investment club was committed to 10 years of building cash. The family invested monthly until enough money was accumulated. During the cash accumulation phase, Barbara took it upon herself to learn how to make money from buying and selling individual stocks and mutual funds. She learned the investment business by going to the library reading investment books, attending investment seminars and workshops.

What are you willing to do to make your dreams come true?

Step 2 Investing: After the cash accumulation phase came the stock investment phase. Barbara learned the investment game well. She was good and began making trades online dramatically growing our investment funds. Periodically Barbara Jean would provide the family with financial reports letting us know how the investments were doing.

From March of 1987 to December of 2007, their family members invested $25.00 each month in the family's future. Barbara became an experienced investor and successfully made steady income for the family investment club.

As phase two was coming to a close it was time to move into phase three of the journey; to establishing a generational family legacy vision. Now that the family had some land and cash, it was time to move into phase three, starting a family business.

As phase two ended their adult children still were not aware of their parents overall vision. They were not aware of their parents vision at this time because their dream had not become a family vision yet. It had not become a family vision because they had yet to write it down and communicate their dream to the next generation.

Are you willing to make personal sacrifices for the greater good of future generations?

Secret Steps To Creating Our iFamily Vision
4th: Start a family investment club.

Vision Tips
Tip 5: Do not wait for all your family members to invest because you may never start.
Tip 6: Invest with the mindset of not withdrawing your investment for at least 5-10 years.
Tip 7: Obtain the education, skills and training needed to successfully implement your family vision.
Tip 8: Develop a legal structure for your investment club and establish written rules to increase your chances of success.

There are those that look at things the way they are and ask why? I dream
of things that never were, and ask why not?
Robert F. Kennedy

Invest, Secure, and Finance the Vision

Invest your time to investigate the steps to secure the future for
the generational blessings.

Commit to a life of high morals and values

Therefore the example is set

Secure in your heart the word of the Lord

The word of God is your security of success

Plan and save your money to finance the vision

Think big and out of the box with clarity and assurance

By
Vanessa Patterson

Family Member Testimonial

Having a family vision means a lot to me. It gives me tremendous hope knowing:

- I am leaving a legacy for our children.

- I have something to look forward to today, tomorrow and in the future.

- I will have a family home place to go to and relax is reassuring. Knowing that we will own it reminds me of the saying "The Sky Is The Limit".

- I can leave an inheritance for my children and grandchildren which my parents were not able to do for me.

If my parents had a vision I can only think how better off we could have been. Working in unity with my family towards the vision is a big step and exciting. I am looking forward to the journey.

Thank you Dr. Porter & Mother Porter for obeying God and leaving us a vision to guide us.

Marilynn Wells
Generations United Board Member
GEN 2

Chapter 3

The Dream Seed Becomes A Bigger Vision

Date	Family Milestones
1/9/2008	The decision to create a family Limited Liability Company and transfer the Colorado property into this family LLC business was made by James & Barbara Porter
1/26/2008	The Porter Family business was given a name Generations United, LLC
3/14/2008	Created a family Vision & Mission Statement
3/28/2008	First inter-generational family business meeting with children and grandchildren held. Our parents dream of building a family resort on the vacant land in Colorado was formally revealed to the entire family.
5/16/2008	Grandson, James, III created a family shield/logo
7/10/2008	Sons Ron Porter & Phillip Porter met with a local law firm to set Generations United as a limited liability company.
7/15/2008	Founded Generations United, LLC
7/23/2008	Sons Ron Porter and Phillip Porter met with our attorney to legally transfer Colorado property into Generations United, LLC.

8/15/2008	Legally transferred the family's investment club assets into Generations United, LLC.
8/22/2008	The Porter Family Vision Photo – The Porter Family Colorado Resort
8/31/2008	Transfer Colorado property into Generations United, LLC completed

There will be a time when your dream will seamlessly transform into a clear vision and mission for your entire family. For the Porter family, that time was in January 2008 when Rev. James and Barbara Porter now 77 decided it was time to officially move into phase III. Remember in phase I, they purchased vacant land in Colorado and were the only ones who clearly knew their dream to establish a home place in Colorado. In phase II, they launched their family investment club and asked the next generation to invest in the family. In this phase II, they still did not reveal their vision for the family.

Now ready to move their family into phase III, James and Barbara believed the family needed to start a family business that will generate enough capital not to build just a home but build a family resort in Colorado. During phase II their vision to build a home on the Colorado property grew to a family resort. Thus the idea of a family business was borne as means to achieve their vision. They believed that only a family business would be able to generate enough capital required to build a beautiful family resort. The announcement of establishing a family business was significant because it included the way they would share their entire dream with the second and third generations.

The launch of phase III began on March 28, 2008 during their first inter-generational family business meeting held at Phillip and Janice's home. Many of their children and grandchildren attended this meeting. This was the first time many family members heard the vision their parents and grandparents had for the family. This action of sharing their dream is when their dream seamlessly transformed into a laser focused vision and mission for the entire family. Until now, their dreams were just that a dream, but now their dream was being transformed into an "Immediate Family Vision" (iFamily Vision) which gave the entire family specific directions. They believed their vision was God inspired so it didn't matter if each family member immediately caught their vision. They believed it was their job to share the vision with the family and it was each family member's choice to receive, ignore or reject their vision. Rev. Dr. James Porter always said that "sharing your vision with the family is like extending the open door to Jesus Christ at church". As a minister, he said "it was his job to extend the open door and it was each individuals job to accept or reject the invitation. If they accepted it, praise the Lord, if they rejected it that is their choice. This same principle applies to sharing your family vision with your entire family. Some will accept it and some may not but either way, God is good."

In order to achieve our iFamily vision, Rev. Dr. James and Barbara Porter launched Generations United.

During a family business meeting, the family agreed with their parents and grandparents dream to build a family resort in Colorado. To achieve this vision, the family agreed to:

- Close the family investment club and transfer the assets into our family business.

- Launch the family's first business that would own the land in Colorado.

- Began to brainstorm to determine the products and services the Company would sell to generate enough revenue to achieve the dream of building a family resort in Colorado.

After the family business meeting there were two tasks to complete. One task for the family and the other task was for the family business.

The family tasks were to:

- Create a formal iFamily vision and mission statement

- Create a family shield

- Select a vision photo

The family business tasks were to:

- Select a Legal Business Entity

- Select a name for our family business

- Determine the product and services our family business would sell

- Create a business vision and mission statements

- Create a business logo

The Porter Family's primary family tasks, were to create the family vision and mission statements; which they began immediately.

Create an iFamily Vision & Mission Statement

The next step to convert their parents dream to a vision was to create written iFamily Vision and Mission Statements. Rev. Dr. James and Barbara Porter charged their son Phillip with the task of creating a written vision statement and mission statement for the family based on their dreams and values. Phillip accepted this major responsibility of writing his parents dreams in a manner that would be clearly understood and communicated to the entire family.

A vision statement outlines what they wanted to accomplish and how they wanted to be known by the extended family, community and world. It gave all the members of their family a clear concise verbal picture of the destination of the family in the future. It had a long-term view for the family concentrating on the future. We define long-term as 10 years or longer. A mission statement is short-term and concentrates on the present fundamental purpose of the family, succinctly describing why the family exists and what it does to achieve its vision.

As a business advisor Phillip has written and helped write hundreds of vision and mission statements for his business students and clients. It was standard business 101 for businesses to have a vision and mission statement. However, he had not written a family vision and mission statement. For the first time, Phillip was wondering why their family never had a vision and mission statement. Even in the bible, ***Proverbs 29:18: Where there is no vision, the people perish: but he that keeps the law, happy is he.*** (American King James Version). So, if this is true and you replace the people with family, then it reads "Where there is no vision, the family perish... Wow! For the first time Phillip truly understood what his dad and mom were trying to implement for the entire family. With this he said "let's get to work and create Godly vision & mission statements for the family".

To create a great vision and mission that would touch the souls and hearts of our family and compel them to action, Phillip had to first interview his parents in order to get a clear understanding of their dreams, goals, personal values and what they wanted to pass down to future generations. After kitchen table interviews and conference calls with his parents there were four values and principles identified that they wanted to pass on. Throughout his life, his parents would express their dreams for their family but never were their dreams written down in the form of a plan. His parents dreams for their family were based on four core values.

Family Core Values

- **Spiritual:** James and Barbara have been Christians for over 60 years and it was their dream that their entire family for all generations would have a strong and healthy spiritual life. The family nurtured their spiritual faith through attending Sunday School and worship service regularly.

- **Education:** Rev. Dr. James Porter who had earned a doctoral degree and Barbara who was a Register Nurse believed education was an essential key to their family's generational success. Rev. Porter always said "if a man wrote it, you can learn it"; meaning you can learn anything. There is nothing too hard for God... Jeremiah 32:17.

- **Health:** Barbara was a nurse for over 30 years. She instilled the value of preventative health care in the entire family.

- **Wealth:** To live in this world you must have money. However, you never put your desire for money before the Lord. Barbara was instrumental in starting their family first investment club as they consistently paid their tithes to the Lord. They purchased 28 acres of land in Colorado and dedicated the land to God for the sole purpose of passing it on to their children. James and Barbara never made any plans to live on this land.

After, Phillip completed the interview with his parents, the family and business, had their first vision and mission statements:

Our iFamily Vision Statement
To build family resorts in several locations throughout the United States that meets the spiritual, physical, educational and financial needs of the family.

Our iFamily Mission Statement
To increase the quality of life for each generation more than the previous generation by: • building upon our rich spiritual heritage • living a healthy lifestyle • pursuing higher education • enjoying regular family reunions • making/increasing financial investments • starting and acquiring businesses • purchasing real estate investments • generating profits and financial independence for the family

The second family task was to create a family shield which reflected our family values, vision and mission.

The Family Shield & Business Logo

To create a family shield/business logo, Phillip interviewed his mom to determine what she would like to see in a family shield.

Three Stars (Dual Meaning):

- **Spiritual**

   ○ God The Father

- ○ God The Son

- ○ God The Holy Spirit

- **Family**

  - ○ Middle Star - Generation 1

  - ○ Left Star - Generation 2

  - ○ Right Star - Generation 3

Light Rays:

- Represents God sending down his blessings and protection

Cross:

- Spiritual Heritage

Man:

- Our burning desire to live a healthy lifestyle and exercise

Three Books (Dual Meaning):

- Wisdom/Knowledge

  - ○ 1st Book - Bible

  - ○ 2nd Book - Prayer Book

  - ○ 3rd Book - Business Record Keeping Book

- Pursuit of Higher Education

  - ○ 1st Generation (G1's)

  - ○ 2nd Generation (G2's)

○ 3rd Generation (G3's)

Gold Bricks in Stair Step Formation

● Building long-term wealth for the business & family

Grandson, James III took this information and created the family shield/business logo. On 5/16/2008 James III presented a logo to the family and it was unanimously approved. His grandparents were overjoyed to see their vision coming alive in the family shield.

Now it was time to work on family business tasks. Their first task was to determine the legal entity for the family business.

Select a Legal Business Entity

The first legal step in making their parent's dream a reality was to establish a family business that would own the Colorado property. This was a high priority for Rev. Dr. James & Barbara Porter, Sr. because they had to protect the land that they worked so hard to acquire from being lost by any one family member including themselves. Rev. Dr. James Porter, Sr. really believed that a person must always know in their heart and mind that if they lost all their personal possessions for whatever reason, they always had a place to stay. When a person loses all hope, the reason for living is also lost. Even the most faithful can lose hope if the right set of circumstances fall upon them. Not many Christians have the faith of Job as stated in the bible.

After getting directions from their father, sons Ron and Phillip consulted with an attorney and Certified Public Accountant, to determine the best legal business entity for the family business. Based on their consultation, the family decided to form a Limited Liability Company for the following reasons:

- Limited personal liability for the owners

- "Pass-through" taxation to individual family members

- No limit on the number of stockholders

- No restrictions on subsidiaries unlike an "S" corporation

- Less burdensome governance requirements

After the decision to form a LLC as the business entity, it was time to name the family business.

Select a Business Name

Under Barbara's leadership, they had several brainstorming sessions. In each discussion she used the word of God, "Bible" as her inspiration to help us come up with a name for our family business.

On March 28, 2008 Barbara made a decision and ultimately the family unanimously voted on the name Generations United, LLC. On July 15, 2008 the Porter Family officially launched Generations United, LLC in Minneapolis, Minnesota. Rev. James and Barbara Porter's dream now had a name in

Generations United, LLC.

Once a formalized family business was established, the first order of business was to transfer the Colorado property from various family members name into Generations United, LLC. Upon completion of this transaction, James and Barbara were at peace knowing that the property purchased in Colorado many years ago would remain under the control of the family business and not in the control of any individual family member including themselves.

As their family and business grew and prospered they would reflect on their vision and mission statements. Their vision and mission statements were living documents guided by God. As God blessed their family and expanded their dreams they revised their vision and mission statements. They believed it would keep each generation engaged and motivated to achieve a goal greater than themselves.

Vision Photo

In August 2008, Phillip began searching for a Porter Family Vision Photo. One that would represent his parent's dream and reflect the vision and mission Statement. Phillip narrowed the photos down to 3 and then asked his son Derek to pick one. Unknowingly, Derek selected the exact same photo Phillip had chosen. Later, Phillip showed the *vision photo* to his parents. This became a mile marker moment in that it was the first time his father seen an actual photo of his dream! This was the first time Phillip had ever seen his father speechless to the point of tears. After seeing the photo, Phillip's dad didn't say a word... Phillip wasn't sure if his father loved or hated the photo of his dream. Then, suddenly Phillip's mom spoke lovingly, passionate and firmly, "James this is it, this is our dream for our Colorado property!". Dad finally spoke and said "yes, it truly is". For the first time in 36 years since the purchase of their land in Colorado, they saw a photo that was a visual representation of their Godly dream. They now had a vision photo that they can share with their children and grandchildren. This was a precious unforgettable moment for Phillip, he will never forget it.

Secret Steps To Creating Our iFamily Vision
5th: Held a family meeting to reveal family vision.
6th: Created a written iFamily vision and mission statement based on the family core values, beliefs and dreams.
7th: Created a family shield to represent the vision and mission of the family.
8th: Started a family business Generations United, LLC with rules and by-laws.
9th Selected a vision photo.

Vision Tips
Tip 9: Make sure the business has rules and by-laws and that require each family member to follow in order to reap the benefits of the business.
Tip 10: The family vision must have individual appeal with an extended family impact.
Tip 11: Continue to share the family vision with the family, to increase family members catching the vision over time.

The Promise

We leave with the assurance of God's promises for our seeds. We taught, lead, guide and lived before our children a Godly life and example. We taught them to "honor thy father and mother that their days may be long".

Exodus 20:12

"Love the Lord your God with all your heart, with all your soul and with all your strength".

Luke 27:10

We repeated the word to you, when we sat at home, when we walked or traveled and even when you went to bed. Furthermore, "Peace I leave you, my peace I give unto you: not as the world giveth, give I unto you. Let not your heart be troubled, neither let it be afraid".

John 14:27

We are confident that the Lord will be with thee, "he will not fail thee nor forsake thee" nor be afraid, remain strong and of great courage.

Deuteronomy 31:6

Remember my children God's word and promise is for you! We are confident that "It shall come to pass, if thou shalt hearken diligently unto the voice of the LORD thy God, to observe and to do all his commandments which I command thee this day, that the LORD thy God will set thee on high above all nations of the earth:

[2] And all these blessings shall come on thee, and overtake thee, if thou shalt hearken unto the voice of the LORD thy God.

[3] Blessed shalt thou be in the city, and blessed shalt thou be in the field.

⁴ Blessed shall be the fruit of thy body, and the fruit of thy ground, and the fruit of thy cattle, the increase of thy kine, and the flocks of thy sheep.

⁵ Blessed shall be thy basket and thy store.

⁶ Blessed shalt thou be when thou comest in, and blessed shalt thou be when thou goest out.

⁷ The LORD shall cause thine enemies that rise up against thee to be smitten before thy face: they shall come out against thee one way, and flee before thee seven ways.

⁸ The LORD shall command the blessing upon thee in thy storehouses, and in all that thou settest thine hand unto; and he shall bless thee in the land which the LORD thy God giveth thee".

Deuteronomy 28:1-8

By
Vanessa Patterson

Family Member Testimonial

Every great ideal starts with a thought, every great thought is the beginning of a great dream and that dream can become a generational goal.

When you connect with other positive people that share your ideals, thoughts, dreams and goals it makes that journey to your vision that much easier. In my case those positive people are my family and my family will never throw me under the bus for their own personal gain. My family allows me to ride the bus to achieve my personal goals under the umbrella of our family's collective vision.

With that being said, I never dreamed I would be part owner of a family company that gives me the opportunity to buy stock for my children. I had the joy of presenting stocks to my children from a company built on the dreams of the generations before us. This was awesome and emotionally overwhelming in so many ways. That company is our family company Generations United, LLC. We all want more for our children than we had growing up. We want to leave them in a better financial position but are unable to do it alone. Due to the ideals, dreams and visions of the generations before us, this dream is a plan and that plan is now a company. I am blessed to be an owner in our family business Generations United, LLC.

Brenda Williams
Generations United Board Member
GEN 2

Chapter 4

The Unlikely Family Merger

Date	Family Milestones
12/16/2012	Phillip Porter interview the leaders of the Williams/Magee family regarding merging the family into Generations United, LLC
12/25/2012	First Extended Family Vision Planning meeting with the Porters/Lamberts & Williams/Magee's in Eagan, Minnesota
12/28/2012	First Extended Family Vision meeting with Williams/Magee family in Tylertown, MS

During the summer of 2009, Phillip's dad's vision for the company and family took an unexpected turn into a direction Phillip did not and at the time could not fully comprehend. It all began during one of their many kitchen table discussions when seemingly out of the blue Phillip's dad totally caught Phillip off guard when he said, "Phil, aren't' you and your wife Janice one?", Phillip said yes sir; then he repeated and said it again, "Phil, aren't you and Janice one?", Phillip said again, yes sir. Phillip had no idea where his dad was going with this question to which he already knew the answer. But later, Phillip would learn the questions were for his benefit not his dad's. Then he said, "Phil, I would like you to merge the Williams

Family into Generations United because you are one with her family just the way she is one with the Porter family. This merger will be first of many mergers into Generations United. All of our children and grandchildren's spouses family's plus cousins, aunts and uncles and their families, can become a part of the business if they see our vision and are willing to follow the rules. But before you do it, I want to reiterate that you must make sure Generations United has solid rules and by-laws in place so everyone can be blessed." Phillip said "yes sir" but did not have a clue why he wanted to do something like this that made no sense. Then finally dad said "Phil, you will know when it's time to merge the families. When the time comes, you do not need my permission" just do it. Phillip said, "Yes Sir". Phillip did not give it any more thought until 2012. Phillip did not share with his wife Janice what his dad had told him because he didn't really understand it himself. At the time Phillip had not clearly seen his dad's complete vision but was doing what his dad asked out of respect and love.

The weeks following Phillip's conversation with his dad, he kept thinking about what his dad said versus what he knew about the key attributes required for a successful business merger. Generally, in a successful business merger, there are crystal clear benefits that both parties will receive as a result of the merger. In many cases, the benefits are so clear, they can be quantified rather easily. However, when his dad told him the final piece of their vision which was to merge the Porter/Lambert family with the Williams/Magee family, the advantages of such a merger was not clear. As a matter of fact, Phillip respectfully thought it was a crazy idea but wisely never voiced this opinion to his dad. Phillip thought the merger would never work because neither family had a successful business, no tangible assets of value, the families don't know each other and the list goes on. Phillip knew just enough to know that God's ways are not our ways and to trust God and his dad's vision. Here are a few facts about the families:

Family Facts

Date	Porter/Lambert Family	Williams/Magee Family
Dad's Name	Rev. Dr. James Porter, Sr.	Willie Lethell Williams, Sr.
Dad's Occupation	Pastor, School Teacher, Author	Steel Mill Welder, Truck Driver, Offshore Oyster Boat
Mom's Name	Barbara Jean Lambert Porter	Elvalene Magee Williams
Mom's Occupation	Deaconess, Nurse, Investor	Choir Member, Mission Ministry, School Bus Driver, Senior Personal Care
Home Town	Gilmer, TX (Kansas City)	McComb, MS (Tylertown)
Date of Wedding	May 1, 1949	December 19, 1955
Number of Children	3	10
Number of Grandchildren	15	39
Number of Great Grandchildren	0	2
Extended Family Size	Large	Enormous
Economic Class	Lower Middle Class	Working Poor
Raised	Urban City	Country

Highly Successful Family Owned Business	No	No

As you see from this family facts list, it's not crystal clear what the benefits each family would receive from such a merger. Plus no one in either family had experience with family mergers. In spite of these facts, Phillip was determined to fulfill his parents request to merge the families.

One day in 2012, Phillip and Janice were discussing how her family (Williams/Magee's) could establish a vision, mission, and an investment club for their family. As soon as their discussion began, Phillip clearly heard his dad's words ringing loudly in his spirit "merge the two families Porter/Lamberts with Williams/Magee's. Until this moment Phillip never thought about what his dad had told him back in 2009. Phillip then asked Janice "what do you think about inviting the Williams/Magee's to become members of Generations United, LLC?" He went on to say, "there is no reason for your family to start from scratch like our family did. We should just join forces together because with greater numbers, we can accomplish more in a faster period of time". Janice immediately thought this was a good idea. This is when Phillip shared with Janice that it was his dad's idea back in 2009 to merge the families. Phillip and Janice were in agreement that they should move forward with his dad's idea to merge the families under Generations United. Even though Phillip and Janice believed this was a good idea, they were not sure what Janice family would say about merging the families. Neither Phillip or Janice had ever been a part of a family merger. This was truly going to be a new experience. They were willing to step out on faith and implement their parents vision to merge the families.

Phillip shared the good news with his dad and his dad was pleased. At this point, Phillip knew and understood with all his heart and mind the vision his parents had for the family. His dad, said "Phil if you say it's time go ahead and do it. Two things must happen before you can merge the families. First the leader of the Williams/Magee family which is Janice's dad Willie Lethell Williams must agree. Second, it must be clearly communicated to the entire family that he agrees. When you are able to accomplish these two tasks, you will know the merger is in God's will. Dad then said, "from this moment on, you no longer need to ask for my permission and guidance because you now know and believe in what our vision is for the family".

This statement was dad's way of passing the stewardship of the family vision to the next generation. When he passed the vision mantel he shared more words of wisdom. These words of wisdom were "even though you believe, understand and have a plan, always leave room for God to intercede in your plan and direct your steps". Phil said "yes sir". With this, Phil along with his wife Janice began to fulfill their parents dream to merge the families. This was a very exciting moment in Phillip and Janice's lives as they have been given the humble opportunity to merge the families.

Phillip and Janice began working on a plan to merge the families into Generations United. They reviewed the company by-laws, policies and procedures. To accomplish this merger, four things had to happen:

- First talk with the family members who were shareholders (unit holders) in Generations United to let them know of the pending merger as directed by our parents.

- Second, talk and get approval from some of Janice's siblings who are the future leaders of the Williams/Magee family. It was important that Phillip and Janice share the vision and the big picture with them and then get their feedback on whether or not this would be a good idea to merge the families.

- The third and most imperative step was talking with Janice's dad to get his approval.

- Finally, issue a press release to notify the Porter/Lambert and Williams/Magee and the community of the merger.

The first week in December 2012, Phillip and Janice notified the shareholders of the family merger. The shareholders all agreed it was a great idea and wanted to proceed rapidly. On December 12, 2012, Phillip and Janice began interviewing some of Janice siblings about the family merger; within 7 days Phillip and Janice had received everyone's approval. This was a great accomplishment.

After receiving approval by the shareholders of Generations United and Janice's siblings, Phillip and Janice decided to announce the family merger at their annual family Christmas Celebration at their home on December 25, 2012.

On December 25, 2012, Phillip and Janice's annual family Christmas celebration became the first eFamily Vision Planning Session and Christmas Party and the event was a great success.

On December 28-29, 2012, Phillip and Janice attended the Williams/Magee Christmas celebration in Tylertown, MS. Phillip and Janice added a family vision session to the family Christmas celebration. This was a big deal because the family never had a family vision planning session as part of the family

Christmas Celebration. Phillip and Janice prayed that the family would be receptive. They knew that having great food would help everyone listen to the family vision for a few hours. By the end of the Christmas celebration everyone agreed that the family merger was a great idea including Janice dad. Phillip and Janice praised God because they were able to see another seed of their parents vision come true. This became a major accomplishment and historical moment which propelled the family forward.

Secret Steps To Creating Our eFamily Vision
10th: Held family meetings to get approval to merge the families.

Vision Tips
Tip 12: If you have a large family let the family leader create the vision and mission statements for the family.

Wisdom to a Clearer Vision

Children consider the ways of the ant and the lilies of the fields. You must consider, think, investigate, and trust in the Lord to make clear to you what is before you. Wisdom is the key to a clearer vision. Children seek wisdom and with the getting get understanding. Job 28:28 says, "The fear of the Lord, that is wisdom; and to depart from evil is understanding". Consider and investigate what you see, what you have to do, what's behind you, what's at hand and what's before you. Think, reflect, and consider the past and all that's gone before you, your present and future generations to come. Have faith in the almighty God that will make the vision clear with guidance and instructions. Consider the vision with openness, possibility, the family unit, and with determination not to be boxed in but free to flow with the blueprint ordained, inspired and designed by the Lord. Children with wisdom from God understanding is a powerful tool to accomplish all that you are destined to become for generations.

By
Vanessa Patterson

Chapter 5

Their Final Chapter Is Our Beginning

Date	Family Milestones
1/4/2013	News Release: Family Merger is Expected To Increase Wealth For Generations
5/20/2013	First Generations United, LLC board meeting with the new board members from the Williams/Magee family
2/14/2014	Generations United, LLC published first book "Journeys To I Do"
11/17/2014	Generations United, LLC launched new line of personalized cases

In January 2013 as Rev. Dr. James & Barbara Porter, Sr. approached the young age of 83, God allowed them to see their promise land through the family merger. The family merger was announced via an official news release which represented first the culmination of a 40 year family vision. Second, the successful transfer of a God given vision to the next generation. Never in their wildest imagination during this 40 years did they believe that their dream seed planted in Colorado for their family would grow and manifest itself beyond the Porter Family to include other families. This is a clear reminder that as visionaries and caretakers of the vision, always leave room for God to bless you beyond your human limitations.

In January 2013, our family issued the following press release:

Minneapolis, Minnesota - Friday, January 4, 2013: The Rev. Dr. James & Barbara Jean Lambert Porter Family and the Lethell & Elvalene Magee Williams Family will merge to establish a joint family generational business under Generations United, LLC. Together the families will utilize their God given spiritual gifts, talents, skills and resources to significantly enhance their spiritual, physical, educational and financial health for current and future generations.

Mission Statement: To increase the quality of life for each generation more than the previous generation by:

- building upon our rich spiritual heritage

- living a healthy lifestyle

- pursuing higher education

- enjoying regular family reunions

- making/increasing financial investments

- starting and acquiring businesses

- purchasing real estate investments

- generating profits and financial independence for the family

2013 will be merger transitional period that is projected to be completed by year end. During this transitional period, Generations United will launch a Facebook Page, Twitter

Account, Blogger or WordPress Blog, website, email, etc. to track family contests, issue family business reports, communicate family activities, and more...

Congratulations to the Porter/Williams/Lambert/Magee Families for coming together and establishing and implementing a godly "Family Legacy Vision Plan" that will guide the family for generations. *Proverbs 29:18: Where there is no vision, the people perish: but he that keeps the law, happy is he.*

For more information contact generations 2s:

Servia Fortenberry, Mable Hewitt, Janice Porter, Phillip Porter, Ron Porter, Marilynn Wells, Phillip Wells, Alex Williams, Brenda Williams, Carlene Williams, Lester Williams, Marvin Williams

By Phillip S. Porter, MBA, President
Generations United, LLC
Gunitedone@yahoo.com
www.facebook.com/GenerationsUnitedLLC
www.unitedgenerations.blogspot.com

Since, Rev. Dr. James and Barbara Porter, Sr., went home to be with the Lord in Heaven, their children and grandchildren collectively are committed to achieving their vision. God continues to expand the family vision the same way He expanded their parents vision over 40 years ago. They know that hard work, sacrifice, communication and trust are the key ingredients to keeping the family vision alive and moving forward through generations. The eFamily vision took a giant leap forward in 2015. The greatest chapter is yet to be written and will be shared in the next book: The Power in a Vision Driven Family II.

Rev. Dr. James & Barbara Porter, Sr. never had the financial resources to build a home on the land but they had the foresight to build a family vision for the land in the hearts of their offspring. It is now the goal of the second and third generations to make their parents and grandparents dream come true with God's guidance.

The family would not have achieved so many great things without the godly vision of Rev. Dr. James & Barbara Porter, Sr. Their eFamily vision and mission statement has:

- Given the family direction. The family has a common goal that drives the family to succeed.

- Given the family hope. Their parents vision gave the next generation a glimpse into their future to see the possibilities via the family vision.

- Given the family better communication. The family now communicates more through family meetings, conference calls, Facebook, Twitter, blogs and more.

- Given the family a formal method of documenting answered prayers.

Secret Steps To Creating Our eFamily Vision
11th: Transferred the stewardship of the vision to the next generations.

Vision Tips
Tip 14: Schedule regular family meetings with an agenda that continues to move your family vision forward
Tip 15: Utilize social media to communicate vision updates to the younger generations
Tip 16: Recite the family mission and vision statements at family meetings including family reunions

Generational Prayer

Dear Lord,

Thank you for my children which are gifts from you. Bless, guide and direct their footsteps on this life journey. Help us to never forget to "train up our children in the way they should go: and when they are old, they will not depart from it".

Proverbs 22:6

Listen, son, to your father's instruction and do not forsake your mother's teaching "My son, do not forget my teaching, but let your heart keep my commandments, for length of days and years of life and peace they will add to you. Let not steadfast love and faithfulness forsake you; bind them around your neck; write them on the tablet of your heart. So you will find favor and good success in the sight of God and man.

Proverbs 3: 1-4

Help us Lord instill in them that they are a chosen race, a royal priesthood, a holy nation, a people for his own possession, that you may proclaim the excellences of him who called you out of darkness into his marvelous light. Teach them to "Trust in the Lord with all your heart, and do not lean on your own understanding. In all thy ways acknowledge him, and he shall direct thy paths."

Proverbs 3:4-6

Instill in them to live in harmony with one another. Help them not be proud and conceited, but be willing to associate with people of low position. Jesus, help them "To be kind to one another, tenderhearted, forgiving one another, even as God for Christ's sake hath forgiven you".

Ephesians 4:32

"May the words of their mouth, and the meditation of their heart, be acceptable in thy sight, O Lord, our strength, and our redeemer."

Psalms 19:14

May they "Seek the Lord and His strength; seek His presence continually".

Psalm 105:4.

Jesus help them "To choose you this day whom they will serve, may they declare as for me and my house we will serve the Lord".

Joshua 24:15

May they be confident in knowing "All things work together for good to them that love God, to them who are called according to his purpose".

Romans 8:28

Jesus help them to "Not be anxious about anything, but in everything by prayer and supplication with thanksgiving let your requests be made known to God".

Philippians 4:6

Jesus help them to "Rejoice always, pray without ceasing, give thanks in all circumstances, for this is the will of God in Christ Jesus for you".

I Thessalonians 5:16-18

Finally, help them as only you can Jesus to "Think on, whatsoever things are true, whatsoever things are honest, whatsoever things are just, whatsoever things are pure, whatsoever things are lovely, whatsoever things are of good report; if there be any virtue, and if there be any praise, think on these things".

Philippians 4:8

"Now unto him that is able to do exceeding abundantly above all that we ask or think, according to the power that worketh in us. Unto him be glory in the church by Christ Jesus throughout all ages, world without end."

Ephesians 3:20-21

"Now unto him that is able to keep you from falling, and to present *you* faultless before the presence of his glory with exceeding joy. To the only wise God our Saviour, be glory and majesty, dominion and power, both now and forever. Amen."

Jude 1:24-25

By
Vanessa Patterson

Chapter 6

Benefits of a Family Vision
By
Vonzella Love Watson

Having a Family Vision; what an awesome idea. When I think about this idea I think of how beneficial it is to have a vision or, as many businesses or corporations call it, a mission statement. As you read in this book, "Without a vision the people perish." Proverbs 29:18 Knowing that businesses, corporations and especially the Bible make these kinds of references to having a vision, helps me to understand how important it must be to have that vision. Having a family vision means that, the family will have a very specific plan to follow when navigating through life. It will enable the family to remain on track even when life situations come up unexpectedly. Finally, having the family vision gives hope, direction and clarity to future generations.

Every organization, corporation, government, nation and religion has a vision. Some call it their mission statement. Others call it their goal statement. Whatever it is called, it is the oil that causes the machine to run smoothly. The benefits in having this vision for the family is something that cannot be measured. The vision offers clear direction.

When a child is born into the family they learn to walk, talk, feed themselves and do things in certain ways. Usually the child will do what the parents do. Even when we are not paying attention to our own actions our children are watching, and nine times out of ten, they will do it the way we do, even if they think they are coming up with unique ideas on their own. So, it is very relevant for us as the parents to have the vision that will direct our actions so that we are leading those children, in the way that is prosperous and enables them to live long.

I am reminded of the scripture in Proverbs that encourages us to train up a child in the way he should go and when he is old he will not depart. Additionally, in Proverbs children are encouraged to obey their parents in the Lord for this is right. It is the first commandment with promise. A child will live long and prosper if he will obey his parents. These benefits cannot be measured. When our vision is grounded in scripture it enables that firm foundation for times when the unexpected happens. One thing we know for sure is that life has many bumps and unexpected turns. When the family has a predetermined vision, this can serve as a firm foundation to turn to, in times when the unpredictable things happen. Our family's core values and beliefs are built on a spiritual foundation which is embedded in the family vision.

For example, when my son was diagnosed with cancer at the age of 17 years old, I knew I could go to God and pray and he had promised that if I asked I could receive. My bible tells me that the effectual fervent prayer of a righteous man availeth much. I turned to the Lord and His word. I put scriptures around the walls of the hospital room and I asked the saints to pray. One night the doctors came to us and they said we don't think he will survive the night. Because part of our family vision was to go to God when trouble comes, that is what I did. I put scripture for healing on all the walls in that hospital room. I got on my face on the floor in that room and prayed throughout the night. While I was praying, my son was coughing and spitting up this black tar like substance until he had a bucket half full of this substance.

Around three o'clock in the morning my son woke up and said, "I'm hungry". I jumped up and called for the nurse. You see no one had really wanted to come in the room up to that point as they did not think he would survive the night. When the nurse got there, she saw he was awake and she emptied the bucket. I told her he was hungry and she immediately ran to get him something to eat. Before we knew it the doctors and nurses kept coming in and everyone wanted to see this boy who was not supposed to make it through the night. Finally, his Doctor said we must call this the healing room because of all the scriptures on the wall and the healing that took place in that room. God had healed this son, Gimal, ("Special Gift from God").

Having that vision, that firm foundation to lead my actions enabled God to step right in as we chose to obey His word and seek his face so He could and would perform the miracle healing and allowed that child to live. In life there are always unexpected things that happen. The vision gives us the road map to follow in the midst of these unexpected situations.

Having the family vision enables direction for future generations. When we see the success that happens during this generation because of the vision, we realize that we must carry on the things that have been successful, for our future generations to be successful. This reminds me of my grandparents and the families they raised.

My mother who is the sister of Rev. Dr. James Porter, Sr. told me time and again about how their father was the founder and organizer of churches. He led his family with the vision he got from the word of God to successfully organize and build a church in his community. My mother would remember the story of how her father led her and her siblings into the church house lined up, single file to go sit on the front row, sit up straight, and pay attention to the word of God. When he was done preaching they would sing and souls would be saved. This family had a vision and it was the greatest vision of all. The vision was for salvation for each family member. I can't help but think that the theme there was to lift Jesus and He would draw all men.

Finally, my mother and her twelve brothers and sisters have carried on the vision implanted in them from their father and we continue to carry that vision on to our children. I look forward to our families continuing to carry this vision on to future generations as it is the best vision I think anyone could have. This vision is for eternal victory.

Chapter 7

12 Golden Key Words To A Family Vision

After many years of traveling on this journey of discovery, implementing and maintaining an inter-generational family vision, the golden keys to the Porter's Family vision have been revealed. Each family's keys to a successful family vision will be different, but some of these essential keys are universal to all families.

Here are the golden keys that unlocked the secrets to Rev. Dr. James and Barbara Jean Lambert Porter's vision.

Faith

Prayer

Action

Communication

Finances

Wisdom

Rules

Knowledge

Persistence

Stewardship

Patience

Tough Love

Chapter 8

The Vision Secrets Revealed

Secret Steps To Creating Our eFamily Vision
1st: Asked God for an "iFamily Vision" that will expand generations.
2nd: Established family's key core beliefs and values.
3rd: Purchased vacant land in Colorado
4th: Started a family investment club.
5th: Held a family meeting to reveal family vision.
6th: Created a written iFamily vision and mission statement based on the family core values, beliefs and dreams.
7th: Created a family shield to represent the vision and mission of the family.
8th: Started a family business Generations United, LLC with rules and by-laws.
9th Selected a vision photo.
10th: Held family meetings to get approval to merge the families.
11th: Transferred the stewardship of the vision to the next generation.

Vision Tips
Tip 1: Establish a grand family vision that is big enough for each individual member and the entire family.
Tip 2: Have enough faith in God & your dream to take action today even if you have to do it by yourself.
Tip 3: Do not procrastinate take action towards your dream today and set an example for your family.
Tip 4: A grand family vision is not achieved without great personal sacrifice.
Tip 5: Do not wait for all your family members to invest because you may never start.
Tip 6: Invest with the mindset of not withdrawing your investment for at least 5-10 years.
Tip 7: Obtain the education, skills and training needed to successfully implement your family vision.
Tip 8: Develop a legal structure for your investment club and establish written rules to increase your chances of success.
Tip 9: Make sure the business has rules and by-laws and that require each family member to follow in order to reap the benefits of the business.
Tip 10: The family vision must have individual appeal with an extended family impact.
Tip 11: Continue to share the family vision with the family, to increase family members catching the vision over time.
Tip 12: If you have a large family let the family leader create the vision and mission statements for the family.

Tip 13: Schedule regular family meetings with an agenda that continues to move your family vision forward.

Tip 14: Utilize social media to communicate vision updates to the younger generations.

Tip 15: Recite the family mission and vision statements at family meetings including family reunions.

Our eFamily Vision Statement

To build family resorts in several locations throughout the United States that meets the spiritual, physical, educational and financial needs of the family.

Our eFamily Mission Statement

To increase the quality of life for each generation more than the previous generation by:

- building upon our rich spiritual heritage
- living a healthy lifestyle
- pursuing higher education
- enjoying regular family reunions
- making/increasing financial investments
- starting and acquiring businesses
- purchasing real estate investments
- generating profits and financial independence for the family

Chapter 9

Your Vision & Mission Statement
(Blank Form Provided)

Your Vision Statement

Your Family Mission Statement

To Invite the Authors of...

"The Power In A Vision Driven Family"
The Journey To A Generational Vision!

"Journeys To I Do"
True LOVE Stories that SURVIVED This & That of Life

"Home, Estate & Property Inventory Management"
A Property Manager's Guide To Home Disaster Preparedness & Inventory Management

To
Book Signings
Facilitate A Marriage Workshop/Conference/Panel
Facilitate A Family Vision Workshop/Conference/Panel
Be A Guest Speaker

Contact
Generations United, LLC
Rogers, Minnesota

Website
https://www.gunitedone.wix.com/phillipjaniceporter

Facebook
https://www.facebook.com/Visiondrivenfamily

Email
visiondrivenfamily@gmail.com

Glossary

1. cFamily Vision & Mission Statement™ (Childless Family Vision & Mission Statements): A cFamily Vision Statement is a clear and concise written statement of where a married couple wants to be in 5-10 years. A cFamily Mission Statement tells the family what they are doing today and how they will achieve their vision. A childless family is comprised of:

- Couple (husband/wife)

2. eFamily Vision & Mission Statements™ (Extended Family Vision & Mission Statements): An eFamily Vision statement is a clear and concise written statement of where elders of the family want themselves and their offspring to be in 5-10 years. An eFamily Mission Statement communicates to the family what they are doing today and how the family will achieve its vision. An extended family is comprised of:

- Parents (husband & wife)
- Grandparents
- Great-grandparents
- Children (adopted, half/step children, etc.)
- Grandchildren (adopted, half/step grandchildren, etc.)
- Siblings
- In-laws (mother, father, brother, sister, daughter and son)
- Aunts
- Uncles
- Cousins

3. iFamily Vision & Mission Statements™ (Immediate Family Vision & Mission Statements): An iFamily Vision Statement is a clear and concise written statement of where elders of the family want themselves and their offspring to be in 5-10 years. An iFamily Mission Statement communicates to the family what they are doing today and how the family will achieve its vision. An immediate family is comprised of:

- Parents (husband & wife)
- Grandparents
- Children (adopted, half/step children, etc.)
- Grandchildren (adopted, half/step grandchildren, etc.)
- Siblings
- In-laws (mother, father, brother, sister, daughter and son)

4. nFamily Vision & Mission Statements™ (Nuclear Family Vision & Mission Statements): A clear and concise written statement of where two married parents want themselves and their offspring (children, grandchildren) to be in 5-10 years. A nFamily Mission Statement communicates to the family what they are doing today and how the family will achieve its vision. A nuclear family is comprised of:

- Parents (husband & wife)
- Children (adopted, half/step children, etc.)

5. sFamily Vision & Mission Statements™ (Single Family Vision & Mission Statements): A sFamily Vision Statement is a clear and concise written statement of where a single person or parents want themselves and/or their offspring (children, grandchildren) to be in 5-10 years. A sFamily Mission Statement tells the family what they are doing today and how the family will achieve its family vision. A single family is comprised of:

- Parent
- Children (adopted, half/step children, etc.)

A motivating family vision statement will inspire your family to dream and a great mission statement will drive your family to action daily. For a family vision and mission to be successful it must be large enough to encompass the personal goals and aspirations of each family member.

Note: A vision statement focuses on the next 5 -10 years but is revised annually to adjust or expand as needed.

ABOUT THE AUTHORS

 **Phillip Sebastian Porter** is an entrepreneur, leader, speaker, author, business advisor, trainer, and loan officer. He has come a long way from his humble beginnings in Kansas City, Kansas to the Chairman and CEO of Generations United, LLC. Under his leadership, Generations United:

- Fulfilled his parents dream and successfully merged the Porter/Lambert with the Williams/Magee family.
- Became a licensed vendor of the United States Marine Corps.
- Collaborated with OtterBox and successfully launched a new line of military smart phone cases.

In March 2005, Phillip co-founded and became President and Chairman with Crystal Treasures, Inc. CTi provides residential and commercial inventory management services to high net worth, high profile and business clients in Minnesota and throughout the United States. Under Phillip's leadership at CTi Home Inventory Services, in 2006, the company received the Friendship Community Services Small Business of the Year Award.

Phillip is the former Chairman of the Executive Board of Directors and Chairman of the Finance Ministry at Greater Friendship Missionary Baptist Church in Minneapolis, Minnesota. He's a former board member of the Dakota County Regional Chamber of Commerce. He was a Quality Manager/Director for Diamond Products Company and Assistant Quality Manager with The Gillette Company.

Phillip is the author of the books The Power In A Vision Driven Family, Journeys To I Do and Home, Estate & Property Inventory Management currently being sold on Amazon.

Phillip was the keynote speaker for the launch of the new Domestic Estate Managers Association (DEMA) Dallas Chapter. He was highlighted in the Brown & Brown Insurance Inaugural Newsletter and the Starkey International Institute Newsletter.

Phillip grew up in Kansas City and attended South Carolina State University in Orangeburg, SC. Phillip received his MBA in Management from the University of St. Thomas in 1987 in St. Paul, MN. He held Property & Casualty Insurance, Life/Health Insurance and Real Estate Limited Brokers Licenses. Phillip has been married to his wife Janice for 31 years. They are the proud parents of three children and grandparent of one grandson. He loves to cruise the Caribbean.

 **Janice M. Williams-Porter** was born in Tylertown, MS and grew up in Progress, MS. She graduated from South Pike High School in Magnolia, MS and attended Jackson State University where she earned a B.S. degree in Biology and a Master's in Science. She earned a Specialist in Education degree from Saint Mary's University in MN. Janice is a doctoral student at Bethel University in Saint Paul, MN, working on her doctorate in K-12 Leadership. Janice has worked in the field of Education for almost three decades as a science teacher and/or administrator in traditional and non-traditional K-12 schools. She's co-founder of Friendship Academy of Fine Arts K-6 Charter School in Minneapolis, Minnesota.

Currently, Janice is a High School Principal in Minnesota. In 2014, Jackson, MS celebrated the 50th anniversary of the Civil Rights Act passing. The city highlighted progress and accomplishments achieved in African Americans lives over the fifty years. This historical event was combined with the largest national celebration of Rev. Dr. Martin Luther King, Jr.'s birthday and legacy. As the first African American Principal in Burnsville, MN and being from the state of Mississippi, Janice was honored by the city of Jackson, MS to serve as the guest keynote guest speaker and Grand Marshall for this combined celebration. She described this event as being, "unforgettable, transformative and a mile marker event in her life". It's an experience she'll pass on to future generations as priceless.

Her passions are God, family, learning and teaching. She's blessed to serve in her church as a Deaconess, Director of the Christian Education Ministry, a Sunday school teacher, and an Executive Board member.

On July 28, 1984 she married her best friend, the love of her life, entrepreneur and author Phillip Porter. They have celebrated 31 blessed years together. They have 3 adult children and 1 grandson.

 **Vanessa Norwood Patterson** is a Middle School Teacher at Jackson Middle School in Jackson, Alabama; she grew up in Thomasville, Alabama and is a 1979 graduate of Thomasville High School. Vanessa embarked upon her scholastic aspirations at Alabama A&M University in Huntsville, Alabama. In 1983, she received her Bachelor of Arts degree in Telecommunications and Business Management. Before teaching, Vanessa worked in retail management with Montgomery Ward, Chicago, Ill. and Target in Minneapolis, Minnesota, and as Office and Sales Manager at Insight News in Minneapolis, Minnesota.

Vanessa has hosted and was co-hosted of two radio broadcast programs: Food for Thought and Nourishment for Soul at

WJDB 95.5 FM in Thomasville, Alabama. And Voices of the African American Community & Tip of the Week on KMOJ 89.9 FM in Minneapolis, Minnesota. Through these programs, she fulfilled a dream to inspire and encourage people to love, honor and respect each other and keep the Lord center in their life.

Vanessa is married to Larry Patterson; she and Larry have been married for nine wonderful years and have two daughters and two grandsons. She is an active member of Kiel Memorial Temple COGIC. Through education and the classroom, she continues the journey of making a difference by teaching, motivating and inspiring the lives of young people. Vanessa loves creative writing, singing, speaking, traveling and spending time with family.

Vonzella Love Watson is a Christian Counselor and Licensed Clinical Marriage and Family Therapist that provides couples, individual and family psychotherapy. She is the owner and CEO of Collaborative Family Solutions. Vonzella is employed with the Department of Veterans Affairs and works at the Kansas City Vet Center as the Marriage and Family Therapist serving Combat Veterans and their families. Vonzella facilitates Group meetings and has organized new groups for the Vet Center. Vonzella participates in outreach events, facilitates the SARRTP (Addiction Group), Briefing at the VAMC and is pioneering Faith-Based outreach events for the Vet Center. Vonzella is also a Licensed Addiction Counselor and Certified in Basic EMDR Therapy.

Vonzella grew up in Kansas City and graduated from Wyandotte High School. She earned an Associate in Science degree from Kansas City, Kansas Community College and a Bachelor degree in Human Relations from Mid-America Nazarene University. Vonzella is a graduate from Friends University with a Master's degree in Family Therapy. She served in the U. S. Air Force. She is a member of The American Association of Christian Counselors and obtained membership at PSI CHI, The International Honor Society in Psychology, as well as, AmeriCorps National Service Network of Volunteers.

She has a strong desire to support and serve her community by helping others. She has served as an organizer of events for the local PTA while serving on the Board as Treasurer and Secretary. Vonzella has appeared on radio broadcast for KGGN 890 AM, Kansas City, discussing topics such as Christian Counseling, Marriage and Family Therapy, and Domestic Violence. Vonzella has also served as a panelist at the Women's conference for Evangelistic Center International Ministries. She has been active in church as a musician, singer, song writer, Sunday school teacher and the Coordinator of her church's New Membership Classes.

Vonzella is a proud parent of four children; each has graduated from high school and some from college and/or technical school. She continues to work with her aunts and cousins maintaining family relationships with both the "Porter and Love" families. It is an honor to be part of this family.

Made in the USA
Middletown, DE
04 October 2016